GAME DAY

Sports Devotionals for Kids

STEVEN MOLIN

Copyright 2000 Cross Training Publishing
Published by Cross Training Publishing
P.O. Box 1541
Grand Island, NE 68802
1-800-430-8588
www.crosstrainingpublishing.com

TO DAD . . .

Contents

GAME DAY

Sports Devotionals for Kids

STEVEN MOLIN

THE FIRST PITCH!

Game One

In the beginning, God created the heavens and the earth...
Genesis 1:1

Think back. Back to the time you first learned to throw a baseball...or the first time you put on a pair of ice skates...or the first time you tried to run a mile. If you can remember it, it was probably an awkward and embarrassing time for you. Beginnings are like that! But just think: if you hadn't begun back then, you wouldn't be as accomplished at throwing, or running, or skating as you are now. Everything we do, we once had to learn.

Maybe you've never studied bible verses before, so now you feel awkward about this. You can't imagine how stuff written 2000 years ago could possibly apply to your life, let alone your sport. But it does! And in these next 50 pages, you will see how the bible—God's Word—will help you, in life and in athletics. There will be sports stories you can identify with, and bible verses you can think about. Each page will contain *Extra Point,* a question for you to ponder and write about. This is your chance to grow...in your attitude toward your sport, and in your faith in God.

When you reach the end of this book, you might even look back over the earlier *Extra Points* and see just how much you've grown. It will be a little bit like looking at scrapbooks from your early athletic days. Don't worry, you'll get better at it!

We start with Genesis 1:1 because it is the very first verse in the bible (Did you know that the word "genesis" means "beginning."?) It's an important verse because it tells us that God is the Source of everything. In the beginning, before anything else was created, God existed. Everything else, he made. He made the sky, and mountains, and trout. He gave Mr. Naismith the idea of basketball! God invented snow for skiing! And God gave you the ability to run, or pitch, or tackle, or putt. God gave you the ability...but you're responsible for developing it! And that's what "Game Day" is all about; developing *you*, and the gifts that God has given you.

EXTRA POINT

What are your greatest athletic abilities? In the space below, write God a thank you note for these abilities, and tell God what you plan to do with them as you grow.

IT'S A
WHOLE NEW DAY!

Game Two

So forgetting what lies behind me, I do my best to reach what is ahead.

Philippians 3:13

The first game of the season is the best! Why? Because last year doesn't matter anymore. If you were undefeated last season, big deal! If you didn't win a game, who cares? In 1991, The Minnesota Twins and The Atlanta Braves met in the World Series. It's the only time a team has ever gone from last place one season to first place the next—and both teams went "from worst to first!" See what I mean? On opening day, it all begins again. Everybody starts with a clean slate!

There something special about the chance to start over. Past failures can now be used as valuable learning experiences. Past victories can bolster our confidence. You're older and wiser, and you've been waiting for this opportunity since last season ended. Now is the time to show how far you've come.

In athletic competition, as in the Christian faith, the chance to start over again is a gift. Because God forgives you for the sins of yesterday, you begin today with a clean slate. And he'll do it again tomorrow. You might have learned some things from the mistakes you made yesterday, but you won't be penalized for that today. It's like a whole new season!

Do your best today! Focus on that which is ahead of you,

not on what's behind you. Keep your eyes fixed on the finish line...not on the starting blocks. It's tough to run straight ahead when you're looking backwards!

EXTRA POINT

In baseball they're called "errors." In life, they're called "sins." Have you learned anything from the errors or sins that might help you in the future? Take a moment to jot down what you've learned.

WHEN THE
GOING GETS TOUGH . . .

Game   Three

I consider that what we suffer at this present time cannot be compared at all with the glory that is going to be revealed to us.

Romans 8:18

Some practices are really tough! Coaches have no mercy! They drive us until we're half-dead. They make us do sprints when we mess up. They don't even care if we're hurt; they make us practice anyway. It isn't fair!

But victory makes it all worthwhile, doesn't it? We forget most of the pain...and the pain we do remember helps us to do it again in preparation for the next game. In the end, we usually admit that all the work was worth it. This is the price we pay for glory.

In life, each of us go through bumpy times, and it seems like life is unfair. A romance ends, or we fail a test, or there is conflict in our family, or there is illness, or there is a death. As Christians, we have God's promise that, in the end, it will all be worth it. But that doesn't make it any easier to endure, does it?

I once heard an Olympic athlete—I think she was a gymnast—say this: "Anything that doesn't kill me makes me stronger." Wow, she's right! It isn't the easy practices that prepare us for the big game, it's the tough ones. And it isn't a cushy life that prepares us for the challenges ahead, it's the struggles that we face...and survive.

Maybe today your life is filled with trouble. Without knowing what your specific struggles are, I can say this: they will end. And when you come out on the other side of them, you will be a stronger person. God is with you, and you don't face this stuff alone. Don't ever forget that fact!

<u>EXTRA POINT</u>

In sports, our coach gives us suggestions for dealing with adversity. Well, God is like The Big Coach, and the bible is like the master playbook. If God were to write a letter to you with ideas of dealing with your life's adversities, what would he say?

ONE
GAME AT A TIME

Game Four

So do not worry about tomorrow; it will have enough worries of its own.

Matthew 6:34

It was a lesson I only had to learn once. We were playing two high school hockey games one week; a real poor team on Thursday, and the perennial league champion on Saturday. We thought we only had to show up in order to win the Thursday game, so we started to think about Saturday. Big mistake! We were beaten badly on Thursday because we looked past it, and we lost the Saturday game, too. Ouch!

This verse from Matthew says two things. The first thing is, deal with what's important today. Not yesterday...not tomorrow...not next week...but today! Maybe you need to make lists to help you prioritize your attention. But there's no sense in solving next week's problems when you haven't yet solved today's. I recently saw this adage and I really liked it:

> **"Yesterday is gone,**
> **Tomorrow isn't yet here,**
> **So today is a gift;**
> **That's why we call it** *The Present!"*

But this verse also tells us something else: it tells us not to worry. Do you know how much energy gets wasted on worrying? And worrying doesn't change anything. This is where God comes in. Tell God your worries. When you pray, give God all the details and all the concerns you have. Then they belong to God, not you! With all the time and energy you save from not worrying, you can use it to solve your problems!

EXTRA POINT

In the space below, list three things that you will need to accomplish in each of the next three days. Refer back to this page later this week and "check" them off when each is completed.

THE
FINISH LINE

Game Five

We are afflicted in every way, but not crushed; perplexed, but not despairing; persecuted, but not forsaken; struck down, but not destroyed.

2 Corinthians 4:8-9

In the autumn of 1968, a story emerged from Mexico City, where the Summer Olympic Games had just been held. That year, the country of Tanzania sent a distance runner by the name of John Steven Akhwari to represent them in the marathon. Early into the race, Akhwari stumbled and severely injured his ankle and knee, but amazingly, he kept on running. The winner—from Ethiopia—crossed the finish line at 7:00 PM, and thousands in Olympic Stadium cheered. Five hours later, Akhwari limped across the finish line, and only the stadium clean-up crew saw it. The next day, a reporter asked the obvious question. "Why did you keep on running, even though you were injured, and there was no chance of victory?" John Akhwari replied "My country did not send me 7000 miles to begin a race; they sent me here to *finish* the race."

Life can be hard. You might face obstacles that seem insurmountable. The goal that you once had may be much more difficult than you ever imagined. Perhaps you are tempted to quit...to give up. It might mean quitting the team, or quitting a job, or quitting school, maybe even this bible study! But by quitting, you will miss out on learning some valuable lessons.

Has God brought you this far in your life just so you'll quit? Or has God brought you here so you'll finish?

The late Jim Valvano, coach of the 1983 NCAA Champion North Carolina State basketball team was nearly dead from cancer. But when he spoke on national television, he uttered these words, and they became the motto for which he is known:

"Don't give up! Don't ever give up!"

The Christian life is like a distance race. You may not win, but that's not the goal. The goal is to finish! Don't give up. Don't ever give up!

EXTRA POINT

This might be one of the harder "extra points." Write a note of encouragement to someone on your team or in your school who needs a pat on the back. Write in here...then re-write it and send it to them. You'll be glad you did...and so will they!

THE GOSPEL ACCORDING TO YOGI BERRA!

Game Six

With people, this is impossible, but with God, all things are possible.

Matthew 19:26

Yogi Berra, the long-time catcher, coach and manager of the New York Yankees and the New York Mets, is known for his wit and wisdom. His sayings even have a name: "Yogi-isms!" Some of my favorites include:

> **"You can observe a lot by watching!"**
> **"50% of baseball is 90% mental!"**
> **"When you come to a fork in the road, take it!"**

But perhaps my favorite Yogi-ism is this simple truth: "It ain't over 'til it's over!" He said this in July of the 1973 season, when the Mets were nine games out of first place. (They went on to win the Divisional Championship!)

Yogi's right, you know. Sports history is filled with stories of amazing comebacks, and games that were won by a team with no real chance of winning. (Our high school baseball coach wouldn't allow us to pack up the bats until the final out, even if we were loosing 17-2.) It ain't over 'til it's over, remember?

This is what faith is! Believing in something that, from the human point of view, is impossible. Jesus once said "It's easier for a camel to get through the eye of a needle than for a rich person to get into heaven." Yikes! Jesus also said "Kill my body and I'll be back in three days." And the people laughed at him! Maybe he was the first to say "It ain't over 'til it's over!"

Just because we can't see something...just because we can't touch it, doesn't mean it's impossible! God can do stuff we can't imagine. God can get us to do things we can't imagine! (He's getting you to read these bible verses, isn't he?) What we call "impossibility," God calls "opportunity!"

EXTRA POINT

Have you ever seen a miracle? If you had to draw a picture of it, what would it look like? Draw it below. (Hey! Nobody else is going to see this but you!)

OKAY, SO THE REFS AREN'T ALWAYS RIGHT

Game Seven

We also boast in our sufferings, knowing that suffering produces endurance, and endurance produces character, and character produces hope, and hope does not disappoint us.

Romans 5:3-5

It was one of the most bizarre basketball games anyone had ever seen... anywhere! In the gold medal game of the 1972 Olympic Games in Munich Germany, the US men's basketball team pulled ahead 50-49 with three seconds to play. The Soviet team inbound the ball, and it was deflected out of bounds with no time left on the clock. End of the game, right? No! The referee said that Russia had called a time out with one second remaining. But then an Olympic basketball official came running on to the court and ruled that three seconds should be remaining. Again, the ball was inbound, the Soviets took a shot and it rimmed-out. The horn sounded, fans filled the court. End of the game, right? No! The same official ruled it had to be done again, with three seconds left. This time, a full-court pass to 6'8" Aleksander Belov resulted in a basket at the buzzer, and USSR wins 51-50.

Sometimes, things don't go our way. Coaches make the wrong decisions regarding playing time, or referees blow a crucial call, or parents treat us unfairly, or teachers just don't understand, or friends abandon us. Whatever! We can respond one of two ways. We can whine and complain and sulk and pout...or we can move on.

The verses above recommend that we move on, and that if we do, positive things can come from our misfortune. Even when we are mistreated, it can teach us patience, and patience will develop character, (Character does Count!) and with character, our trust and reliance upon God deepens. Wow! All this because the ref made a lousy call!

Someone once said "Life is 10% what happens to us, and 90% the way we react to it." I think that's true!

EXTRA POINT

How far back do you have to think to find an example of being treated   unfairly? What happened...and how did you respond? Describe the incident here...

ARE YOU
A MARKED PERSON?

Game Eight

"You have been sealed by the Holy Spirit and marked with the cross of Christ forever."

The Service of Baptism

One of the most grueling of all athletic competitions is The Tour de France bicycle race, held every July in France. The course covers more than 2100 miles in three weeks, much of it over mountainous terrain. Whoever wins this brutal event gains the title "World's Greatest Cyclist."

You always know who the leader of The Tour de France is; he wears a bright yellow jersey. He is clearly marked as the leader; a target for everyone to shoot for as they peddle toward the finish line in Paris. People are watching him... seeing how he reacts under pressure...gunning for him, so to speak. Fall out of first place and he must give his jersey to somebody else, and then he is out of the spotlight.

Sometimes, I think this is what it means to be a Christian. We are marked people, and the world is watching us. People want to know if this "faith business" has any impact on the way we live our lives, especially under pressure. In some cases, people are "gunning for us" because they have felt judged by us, and they want to see us fail. When we fall down, they might even brand us as "hypocrites."

In truth, we have been marked as "special people." In our baptism, God has claimed us as a daughter or a son; a relationship that will last forever. But with that privilege comes responsibility; for the baptismal service goes on to say:

"Let your light so shine before others so that they may see your good works and glorify your father who is in heaven."

Our marking is not a yellow jersey, that can be put on and taken off, depending on our performance on any given day. Our marking is permanent; God sees the mark of baptism on us everyday. But what do the people around us see in the actions of our daily lives?

EXTRA POINT

Someone once posed this question: "If you were arrested for being a Christian, would there be enough evidence to convict you?" Think about your life over the past 24 hours; what evidence...what "light" have you shone to those who might be watching you? List it here.

ALL THE
GREAT ONES KNOW THIS!

Game Nine

Seek first the kingdom of God and his righteousness and all these other things shall be yours as well.

Matthew 6:33

Number 99. Wayne Gretzky, a hockey player that has dominated his sport for so long, he has certainly earned the title "The Great One." Plus, he's a class act! I had the opportunity to skate with him once, and he was very nice, very friendly, and very, very good!

Someone once asked Wayne Gretzky what made him so great, and this is what he said:

> **"Most players go to where the puck is;**
> **I go to where the puck is going to be."**

As young people, we tend to go where everyone else is going. We tend to do what everyone else is doing. We don't want to appear weird or different, so we go with the crowd...even if they're going to the wrong place! It is a very difficult thing, to go against the crowd, even when it seems like the right thing to do.

As Christians, we are not called to be like "most players." We are called to be different, to do the right thing, to stand up for that which we believe, even when it isn't popular or cool. What's important now is not what will be important later. If you can figure out what qualities will be valuable as a young adult ("where the puck is *going* to be!") it will help you develop those qualities now.

So how does "Seek first the kingdom of God" fit into all of this? It's really quite simple; if you try to figure out what God wants you to do with your life, he promises to guide you through all the craziness and—ultimately—bring you joy. But all this means that you've got some choices to make!

EXTRA POINT

I am going to ask you to be critical and judgmental for a moment (not normally a good thing to do!) Think about some of the choices about "lifestyle" that your friends are making. What's good about those choices...and what is potentially dangerous about them?

DON'T
FORGET ELBOW PADS!

Game Ten

Put on the full armor of God...The belt of truth, the breast-plate of righteousness, the shoes of the Gospel, the shield of faith, the helmet of salvation, and the sword of the Spirit.

Ephesians 6:11-18

When I played hockey, I was a goaltender. Standing still, while players blasted 100-mph slapshots past my ear isn't necessarily my idea of a good time, but when I was younger, it was a thrill! Was it dangerous? Not really, because I was wearing all the right equipment—50 pounds of it! It was hard to skate very fast with all that bulk on, but I knew I was safe from flying pucks, sharp skates and slashing sticks.

Did you know that we need certain "equipment" if we're going to be safe as Christian young men and women in this world? (I'm not talking about elbow pads and shin pads, here. It's more subtle than that.) The Apostle Paul, a fellow who lived just after Jesus did, wrote the words above, and they still are good advice today. Paul says we're supposed to wear...

The Belt of Truth There are so many lies and myths about God. Jesus once said "If you know the truth, the truth will make you free." Do you know the truth about Jesus; that he died for your sins?

The Breastplate of Righteousness is this: if you are convinced in your heart that Jesus loves you, it's all you need to know. The breastplate protects your heart!

The Shoes of the Gospel allow you to "*go and tell*" others that Jesus loves them too.

The Shield of Faith protects you when Satan hurls insults at you. (*"If you have to believe in God, you must be a wimp! C'mon, God isn't watching!"*)

The Helmet of Salvation protects our minds from doubt...another thing that the Devil is good at throwing at us! (*"God doesn't really love you. You're too sinful. You have to be perfect."*) Know what you believe! The helmet will protect you.

The Sword of the Spirit allows us to cut through all the lies of the world. Luther, when   he was tempted, would say out loud "I have been baptized!" Now that's a Sword!

By using this daily devotional, by saying prayers, by attending worship, by reading the bible, you are putting on the right equipment to keep you safe!

EXTRA POINT

Which of these "weapons" do you need to further develop? Once you have identified it, brainstorm and jot down 10 words that will help you focus on it.

SOME PEOPLE
CALL HIM "WIZARD"

G a m e   E l e v e n

Therefore, since we have so great a cloud of witnesses sur-rounding us, let us also lay aside every encumbrance, and the sin which so easily entangles us.

Hebrews 12:1

John Wooden, who has been nicknamed "The Wizard of Westwood" was the men's basketball coach at UCLA for 26 seasons. That in itself is amazing! But his success as a coach is probably never going to be equaled:

Ten National Championships: 1964, 1965, 1967, 1968, 1969, 1970, 1971, 1972, 1973, 1975, (Ten in 12 years!) 88 Consecutive victories (the previous record was 60) 38 Consecutive victories in the NCAA Tournament. (previous record was 16) Eight undefeated Pac-10 Seasons (Tough con-ference!)

With all this success, what do you think his secret is? Good motivational speaker? Brilliant basketball mind? Illegal recruit-ing? No, none of this. When asked recently what the key to his success was, Wooden replied

"I believe in the three F's: Family, Friends and Faith."

Truth is, we can't make it alone in this world. No matter how great an athlete we may think we are; no matter how strong, or fast, or tough, we need the three F's to help us sur-vive. That's what The Apostle Paul is saying in the bible verse above. That we have this cloud of witnesses—the family and friends who love us—cheering us along the way. And we have this faith, which allows us to deal with the sins in our lives, so we can become the person God wants us to be.

All the great characters in the bible relied on "The Three F's" in their lives...even Jesus! Hey, nobody is a Lone Ranger in this world! We need God, and we need each other!

EXTRA POINT

Below, make two lists. On the left, list those who are on your "Three F's" list. On the right, whose lists are you on? These are the most important lists in your life!

"Family, Faith and Friends"	I'm on these people's list
1. God	1. God
2.	2.
3.	3.
4.	4.
5.	5.

Keep going if you need more room...

ON
CHEATING . . .

G a m e   T w e l v e

Dishonest gain will never last, so why take the risk?

Proverbs 21:6

C heating in sports: it happens all the time. Pitchers scuff baseballs to allow the ball to move more, power forwards grab the jersey of their opponent when the referee can't see, tackles chop-block, golfers "forget" a putt, sprinters give an elbow on the turn. I'm ashamed to say this, but while coaching youth hockey, I once snuck an extra player onto the ice late in the game. Like I said, cheating happens all the time in sports. And it's wrong!

The writer of Proverbs was probably <u>not</u> referring to sports when he wrote the verse above. (Apparently, cheating happens in other areas of life, too.). But his words so clearly fit the sports scene! When we cheat, it cheapens our accomplishment. We know...and our opponent knows...and God knows that we won, but we had to cheat to do it. That leaves a hollow feeling inside a person long after the game has ended, and if you have ever done it, then maybe you agree with the writer of Proverbs. It's not worth it, is it?

Think for a moment, about all the athletes who are now remembered because they cheated. Pete Rose, the 1919 Black Sox, Ben Johnson, Tonya Harding. You may not know the name Panuta Rosani. She was a Polish shot-putter in the 1976 Olympic Games, but she will forever find her place in the record books as being the first Olympian to fail a drug test.

I think I'd rather be remembered as someone who played and lost than someone who won...and cheated. How about you?

EXTRA POINT

Why do you play sports? Write a three-paragraph answer to the question, but don't answer too quickly. (Think about the question for a moment.)

WITH APOLOGIES
TO AN UNKNOWN SERVANT

Game Thirteen

And so they arrived at Capernaum. When Jesus and the disciples were settled in the house where they were staying, Jesus asked them "What were you discussing along the way?" But they were ashamed, for they had been arguing about which of them was the greatest!

Matthew 9:33-34

The disciples must have been jocks! I say that, because their conversation sounds like a description of so many of the athletic teams I have ever known. The stars, arguing among themselves about who was more valuable to the team. "Here's my point total...Here's how much I can bench-press...Listen to this clipping about me from yesterday's paper!" And now, Jesus' words to those disciples are his words to us: **"Anyone wanting to be the greatest must be the least—and the servant of all!"**

When I was in high school, we had a team manager who ran errands for the coach. He carried the medical kit, he washed the game jerseys, he turned out the locker room lights. We got the headlines and the glory, he picked up dirty towels. I am embarrassed now to tell you that I can't even remember his name! But he is exactly the one Jesus was talking about when he said "The greatest is really the least of all and the servant of all!"

Do you ever take notice of your team's manager? She probably works just as hard as you do. Do you ever encourage the fourth-string players? They might even love the game more than you do! Do you ever say thanks to the assistant coach, or the cheerleaders, or your parents, or the fans. They give you so much attention...what have you given them?

EXTRA POINT

In a recent "Extra Point" you were asked why you play sports. Remember? Think about the manager or that fourth-stringer your team...how do you think they would answer that question? Write "their answer" here, and then compare it to your own.

LIFT
HIGH THE CROSS

Game   Fourteen

**For I am not ashamed of the gospel of Jesus Christ, for it is
the power of God for salvation to every one who believes.**

Romans 1:16

Do you know the story of Dave Dravecky? He was an all-star left-handed pitcher for the San Diego Padres and San Francisco Giants, who pitched eleven innings in the 1984 World Series without giving up a run. So why would Dave Dravecky, in 1990, write a book entitled *Comeback* ? If you have never heard his story, I think his reason for writing the book will surprise you.

In October of 1988, a cancerous tumor was discovered in Dravecky's left arm. (I did tell you he was a *left-handed* pitcher, didn't I?). Half of his deltoid muscle in his pitching arm had to be removed (the deltoid is the muscle in the back of your upper arm). Everyone thought his baseball career was over; after all, he only had half an arm! But ten months later, Dave Dravecky pitched a game in Candlestick Park in front of 35,000 screaming fans, going eight innings and picking up the win. Following the game, a press conference was held, and reporters swarmed the smiling pitcher, firing questions at him. But at one point, Dravecky held up his hand and said:

**"Before I answer any more questions, I have to give credit
where credit is due. I want to thank Jesus Christ, because
without him, there is no story."**

Do you ever give credit to Jesus Christ for your athletic ability? And not just after you win a big game, but how about after losing a big game...or even for playing in the game? If there is something wrong with athletes today, it is that egos have become larger than the playing field. Athletes have forgotten that God is the Source; and the athlete is simply doing what God has gifted he or she to do. You don't have to kneel and pray in the end zone after scoring a touchdown! You don't have to "cross yourself" before a pair of free throws. But shouldn't you acknowledge the One who gave you the gift...and the opportunity to play the game you love so much?

EXTRA POINT

If you were interviewed following a big game, how would you answer this question? "Hey, you played a great game tonight! How can you explain your success?"

I DON'T WANNA BE LIKE MIKE!

Game Fifteen

There is neither Jew nor Greek, there is neither slave nor free, there is neither male nor female; for you are all one in Christ Jesus

Galatians 4:28

If you are a female athlete, your life changed in 1972. You are probably too young to know it, but that is the year <u>Title IX</u> was signed into law, requiring that all schools which receive federal funds dedicate the same commitment to women's sports as they do to men's.

This was huge! Up until this time, very few high schools or colleges had full scale athletic programs for female athletes. Oh, there was gymnastics and track, and Iowa had a pretty good girls high school basketball program. But to most people, sports was a "guy thing." Not anymore!

Just think about all the accomplishments women's athletics have made in these 25 years. Women's college basketball is a great game! Now there's a WNBA. Fast-pitch softball is dominated by women. Volleyball features girl athletes setting, spiking and digging with power and grace. And the USA women's hockey team won the gold!

Why should this surprise us? (I hope you're reading this, guys!) Why should this "female athleticism" surprise us? It shouldn't! For years, women and girls were dismissed or discounted as athletes. But once they were given the opportunity to compete, they have come to compete big time!

It's about time that girls were given sports models to look up to and try to imitate. Mia Hamm, Tami Granato, Annika Sorenstam, and Rebecca Lobo are women athletes that deserve our attention and applause. But more than that, it is time we recognized that God does not spend more attention on guys, God does not gift men with more physical ability, and God doesn't favor one gender over the other. In short, men and women are equal in God's sight. If God thinks so...shouldn't you?

EXTRA POINT

Unfortunately, "the Church" is one of the places where sexism is strongest. Can you think of some roles in your church or in society where females need to be encouraged? List them here.

YOUR OFFERING

Game Sixteen

I urge you therefore, brothers and sisters, by the mercies of God, to present your bodies as a living sacrifice, holy and acceptable to God, which is *your offering*—an act of worship.

Romans 12:1

hen John Elway, the quarterback of the Super Bowl champion Denver Broncos, announced that he would return for the 1998 season, the fans rejoiced! There had been much doubt, because of all the abuse Elway's body has sustained over 15 NFL seasons. I recall a television interview with Elway last winter, in which he said:

"It used to be, I could play a game on Sunday, take Monday off and be ready for practice Tuesday. A few seasons ago, I rested until Thursday. Now, my body is so sore, I'm lucky to practice by Friday...if at all."

It's safe to say, Elway sacrifices his body for the team. He stays in the pocket and gets sacked in an attempt to complete passes. He gets tackled by guys who weigh twice as much as himself, scrambling to pick up a first down. "Take one for the team!" That's what Elway has been doing all these years. In a way, I suppose this is a sort of "living sacrifice."

Paul, who wrote Romans, suggests that we do something like this for God. He wants us to present ourselves as a <u>living sacrifice</u>. (In the Old Testament, lambs would be cut up into pieces and placed upon the altar. The problem is, they were dead!) God doesn't want us dead; God wants us to be alive...with a personality... with choices...with freedoms.

So what does it mean to be a *living sacrifice?* It means that we set aside our own wants and wishes, our own selfish dreams and schemes, and live our lives the way we think God wants us to live. It might mean avoiding drugs, or sex, or alcohol, or crudeness. Like John Elway, we might take some abuse from people. Staying sober, or pure, or drug-free, or clean-mouthed might sometimes seem like we're being forced into acting religious. Hey, not at all! That's the thing about *living sacrifices:* they can crawl off the altar anytime they want to! But Paul says that when we choose to live the way God wants us to live, it's like our offering...a way we can say "thanks" for the forgiveness of our sins.

EXTRA POINT

What's your "living sacrifice" been for God? What kind of offering have you given in the past month?

ARE YOU A "MARATHON MAN"?

Game Seventeen

Let us run with endurance the race that is set before us.

Hebrews 12:1

I t is no coincidence that the distance of a marathon race is 26 miles, 385 yards. Let me tell you the story of its origin....

In the year 490 BC, the Persians attacked the Greeks on the "Plains of Marathon" which is about 25 miles from Athens. According to the legend, when the battle ended, a runner named Pheidippides brought the news to the people of Athens. The distance from Marathon to the stadium in Athens? 26 miles, 385 yards! When he arrived, he yelled "Rejoice! We conquer!" And then he died.

There are some interesting parallels between the marathon and the Christian life, I think.

The first is this; it's a long journey over rough terrain, and sometimes we might wonder if it's all worth it. In the marathon, the joy of running across the finish line is what drives its participants. In our faith, it's the fact that we get to be with Christ when this life is over.

In the marathon, the runner must pace herself, or she will not have enough energy to complete the race. The same is true for the Christian life; a steady pace of growing in our faith is better than sudden religious sprints, followed by periods of dryness that can discourage us.

But most importantly, in that first marathon, Pheidippides left nothing on the course! He spent everything...every ounce of energy in the race. In our Christians lives, we ought to live in such a way that we have no regrets. One of the saddest things a person can say (in sports or in life!) is "I wish I would have...."

You are engaged in a marathon race, right now! The competition is not the other runners; they're on your side! The competition is getting to the finish line and giving it your very best along the way. Do that in sports! Do that in life! Do that with Christ, and you will be able to say "Rejoice! We conquer!"

EXTRA POINT

As you look back over your young life, do you have any regrets? (Think hard!) If you do have a regret, is there a way to change it now? Write a plan, and then set about reversing that regret.

NOW
THIS IS SPECIAL!

Game Eighteen

And be kind to one another, tender-hearted, forgiving each other, just as God in Christ has also forgiven you.

Ephesians 4:32

hortly after the Summer Olympic Games left Atlanta in 1996, The Special Olympics came to town. Perhaps you've heard of "The Special Olympics." They are competitive games for those athletes who are physically or mentally challenged in some way, and yet still have an athletic talent and a desire to compete. Anyone who has ever been involved with this competition says that everything about it is special!

Pastor Frank Harrington describes a scene he witnessed in the running of the 100 meter dash. They were all lined up on the starting line, ten-year olds, with their eyes on Olympic gold! The gun sounded and they were off, but after just a few feet, a runner fell. Hearing him scream, one of the other racers turned around and saw him lying there, so she went back to help. Noticing this, so did another runner, and another, and another. Pretty soon, everyone had stopped running! Together, they helped that injured athlete to his feet, and all of them walked(!)...they walked across the finish line together!

I am not suggesting that you try this in your next race! (Coach wouldn't understand this one!) What I am suggesting is that this lesson...a lesson taught to us by a group of "specially challenged" athletes, is that sports is more than just beating our opponents. It might also be about caring for those who share the race with us. It might be about drawing the best from ourselves, instead of simply being good enough to beat someone else. Because when beating our opponent becomes the most important thing in sports, it doesn't end there. Unfortunately, we carry our competitive spirit off the field, or off the court or track, and into the rest of life. And then our classmates or our family members or our neighbors become "the enemy" instead of our sisters and brothers.

Learn kindness! Use athletics to develop a sense of accomplishment, rather than a sense of superiority. And finally, realize that Jesus died for the person in lane number 7, same as he did for you. How can you dislike him so, when Jesus loves him?

EXTRA POINT

Do you think you treat people any differently, because you are a Christian? If so, write about it here. If not, do you think Christians should live any differently?

THAT DOESN'T
MEAN YOU'RE A LOSER!

G a m e   N i n e t e e n

I looked throughout the earth and saw that the swiftest person does not always win the race.

Ecclesiastes 9:11

eldom do we remember "second place." Tiger Woods won the 1997 Masters Golf Tournament...not sure who finished second! The Denver Broncos won the 1999 Super Bowl...who'd they play again? Tara Lipinski won the women's figure skating gold, but what about the bronze and silver? You see, we live in a world that only remembers winners (and even them we soon forget!).

But the best person or the best team doesn't always win. One bad game...or one bad pitch...or one skate edge that doesn't hold, and we're done. It doesn't necessarily make us second-best, and it certainly doesn't make us "losers!" This is a good thing for us to remember, because when we finish second (or lower) we still have value. But it is also important for another reason: when you beat your opponent, they still have value, too! You may have won today, but tomorrow it might turn out differently.

This carries over into our daily lives. When we don't get the job we had hoped for, or the "right guy or right girl" for a date, or when we don't do as well as we planned to do in a test, it doesn't make us bad people. Instead of feeling defeated or devalued, put a positive spin on it and learn something from it. I can tell you this much; I have learned more from the failures in my life than I have in the successes. You might ask yourself if that's true for you?

But in all of it, know that, to the people who really matter, it doesn't matter! God loves you, your parents love you, your friends care about you, and you respect yourself. If you learn this important lesson, you can never really lose!

EXTRA POINT

This may seem a bit cheesy, but take five minutes and write as many "self-compliments" you can think of. Again, nobody but you is going to see this, so...be generous and conceited...just for this time!

TEAMWORK!

Game Twenty

For just as we have many members in one body and all the members do not have the same function, so we, who are many, are one body in Christ.

Romans 12:4-5

One of the things that makes football such a great game is the necessity of teamwork. As good as a quarterback's arm may be, he's not throwing any passes if he doesn't get good blocking. No matter how quick the running back is, it takes the powerful linemen to open up the holes. It seems like the players in the glory positions get all the headlines (the QB's, the wide receivers, the free safeties). But they will be the first to tell you that it's the guys in the trenches that are the unsung heroes (the linebackers, the nose guards, the tackles and the tight ends). Fact is, they are all important, and if any one of them doesn't do their job, the play breaks down.

And that's the church! Oh, the preachers and the organist and the song team might get the spotlight, but the church (which we sometimes call "The Body of Christ") is all of us. You are just as important as the preacher. Your friends, who may not be able to carry a tune in a bucket, are just as valuable as the choir. If you didn't contribute your talent, or your ability (whatever it is!) it makes the church like a football team playing with just ten players.

What if the left tackle were to say "I think I'll let this guy past me this play." The quarterback gets sacked! "What if the holder were to think "I wonder what would happen if I just let the snap hit me in the helmet?" A field goal gets missed! But this sort of thing happens all the time in the church, when people don't use the gifts God has given them. And that's sad.

In the church, we have a fancy name for this; it's called "stewardship." It involves using the gifts God has given to us. If God gifted you with the ability to throw 90 mph fast balls, wouldn't you use that gift as a pitcher? If God gave your sister the ability to kick a soccer ball 50 yards, wouldn't you be upset with her if she didn't play on a soccer team? Then how do you suppose God feels, when he has given you gifts that could be used in his church, and you don't bother to use them?

EXTRA POINT

What do you have to offer the church? Are you a singer? Can you usher, or teach Sunday School, or fold bulletins? Are you a team player in your congregation?

LOSERS
AND WINNERS

Game Twenty-One

But many who are first now will be last then; and some who are last now will be first.

Matthew 19:30

s a sixth grader, I recall seeing it; it was hiding there in the trophy case of the local high school that I would one day attend. As I would stand there and study the names on the MVP trophies, and the All-American certificates, and the state championships, this framed poem seemed so out of place.

When the One Great Scorer comes to mark against your name It matters not that you won or lost, but how you played the game

Grantland Rice-

Now, let me say this; winning is important. Otherwise, we wouldn't have scoreboards! But at the youth level, winning has become way too important. I know all the clichés:

"Winning isn't everything, it's the only thing!"
"Show me a good loser and I'll show you a loser!"
"Nice guys finish last!"

But Grantland Rice's poem...right there in the trophy case...says something about God's attitude toward winning the

48

game. He doesn't care! Fifty years from now, it will not matter who won. But it will matter if you learned sportsmanship. It will matter if you developed your God-given talents to the fullest. Sorry to say it this way, but God doesn't care if you win or lose!

EXTRA POINT

Do you "know" any of your opponents? How do you feel about them?   Like them or hate them? Respect them or not? List a few of their names here, and write some complimentary remarks about them. And while you're at it, what do you think they would say about you?

FAITH
EQUALS STRENGTH

Game Twenty-Two

I can do all things through Christ who strengthens me.
Philippians 4:13

Do you ever feel inadequate? I'll bet you do. It's part of growing up; wondering if you can really cut it, when everyone else around you is so talented. When we move to each new level of competition, the feelings start all over again. You might look at the others and question if you even belong. One guy said it this way: "Did you ever feel like the world is a black tuxedo, and you're a pair of brown shoes?"

I have two thoughts for you regarding the feelings of incompetence or weakness.

The first thing is this; it's not just when you are growing up that you feel this way! There are people in their 30's, 40's and 50's who wonder if they can compete against those around them, the ones who look so talented and act so confident. It's human nature to compare ourselves to "the competition" and feel like we come up short.

The second thing is this; everybody else around you is thinking the same thing! Oh, they may hide their feelings of fear or incompetence (just like you are hiding yours!) but it's there. And they look at you and think "Wow! That girl has it made!"

The verse above tells us that, if we trust God, God will fill us with strength. "What kind of strength?" you ask. Strength to make the team?...strength to win the game?...strength to hit

.400, or shoot a 72, or score 30 points? **No! You're aiming too low!** What God will give you the strength to do is to do your best! The power to change! The ability to become greater with him than you could be on your own. The opportunity to win the respect of your teammates and your opponents. The ability to exhibit faith when everyone else exhibits fear. God will give you strength to go on, even when the future looks grim, and all the front-runners have left you in the dust. Then you will pray this prayer of trust and hope: **"I can do all things through Christ who strengthens me."** Because you can!

EXTRA POINT

Are there areas of your life where you feel uncertain or inadequate right now? List them here, and imagine (and write!) how Christ might strengthen you in these situations. He can do it through you!

REACHING
FOR THE PRIZE!

G a m e   T w e n t y - T h r e e

Like an athlete, I punish my body, treating it roughly, training it to do what it should, not what it wants to.

1 Corinthians 9:24

My son was a cross-country runner in college. Watching him train gave me a great deal of respect for the sport and for the runners who compete in it. What I learned in the process of watching him is that, the race is not really won on race day. Whether its a 5K or 10K or a marathon, it's actually won out on the training runs, when the athlete covers many miles, over steep hills and rough terrain, in miserable weather conditions. Although college cross-country races only cover 5 miles, Kyle would commonly run 12 or 15 miles in preparation. He did what Paul describes in the verse above.

In the Christian life, there are some who expect it to be easy. Maybe somebody told them—or they have come to assume—that if you believe in Jesus, you are headed for a cushy life. No problems. No pain. No failures. No disappointments. What I have to tell you today is that nothing could be farther from the truth. We are engaged in a difficult lifelong event. Our faith will place us in situations where we might be bruised and bloody...but that's just preparation for the greater challenges that are coming later.

But all this requires discipline! It calls you to spend time in prayer and thought, about what God wants for your life. It calls you to discipline your lifestyle; athletes treat their bodies with great respect—Christians should, too! And it requires you to always be looking ahead toward the goal...the "prize" as Paul calls it. And what is it? In sports, it's just a trophy. In our Christians lives, it's eternal life with Jesus Christ. Let the training begin!

EXTRA POINT

Discipline doesn't just happen! It takes a plan. Have you ever tried "goal-setting?" List below some goals for the next six months (personal, athletic, academic, spiritual). Remember, A goal must be:

A) **Specific**

B) **Measurable**

C) **Achievable**

JUST DON'T

Game Twenty-Four

And do not be conformed to this world, but be transformed by the renewing of your mind...

Romans 12:2

THERE'S a lot of pressure to "conform" in our world today. You, as young people, are very aware of this. From the way you dress, to the way you talk, to the type of cars you want to drive, to the music you listen to and the colleges you hope to attend. Many choices are made by peer pressure. That's conformity, and it is also very present among adults in our world.

Conformity is not all bad. As part of a team, we commit to dressing in the same uniform (that's called "uniformity"), to act according to the team rules, and to play in a certain way that is the same for all of us. This is healthy conformity. Conformity is unhealthy when it leads us into actions that are potentially harmful, and when it causes us to do things that we would rather not do. Have you ever smoked a cigarette, or looked at pornography, or drank, or chewed, or sworn... just to be cool? That's conformity.

The world would like to conform you! Make you look and act and sound just like everybody else in the world. Advertising is all about "conforming" you into buying their products. If you become "just the same" as everybody else, it's working! Someone once said "If two people are exactly the same, one of them isn't even necessary!"

But God doesn't want you to be conformed...God wants you to be *transformed*. To be transformed means "to be changed." To be different from the world; to set a different standard, and a higher set of principles. And God wants to change you, not just on the outside, (that's conformity, remember?) but on the inside. God wants to cultivate in you new values, new priorities, new attitudes) One of my favorite bible verses is Second Corinthians 5:17:

"If anyone is in Christ, they are a new creation; the old has passed away, the new has come."

God created you to be unique. The world wants us all to be the same. Which way are you headed?

EXTRA POINT

Who are the role models in your life? Don't forget to consider parents, brothers or sisters, friends, teachers, coaches, youth director, athletes, rock stars, TV personalities, etc. List them here, and remind yourself why you want to imitate them.

WAIT
'TIL NEXT YEAR!

Game Twenty-Five

Rejoice in the Lord always! I'll say it again, rejoice!

Philippians 4:4

So we've come to the end of *Game Day*. I hope it has been a good experience for you, that it has caused you to read some of God's Word, but also to try to understand how it applies to your sport and your life. And just because this booklet is over doesn't mean you should stop reading, and praying, and thinking, and growing in your Christian life. Check out overtime at the end of this book. It'll give you some direction for your future.

Remember Game Two? I said that the first game of the season is the best, because we can forget about last year and start fresh and clean. But the last game of the season is different. If we lost a bunch, that still hurts. Ouch! If we won a lot, we hate to see the season end. And it's a long time 'til next year. Either way, we have to sit and wait, and for anybody (but especially for a teen-ager) that's tough. Let me give you something to chew on "off season."

The verse above was written by The Apostle Paul; we've talked about him before. "Rejoice in the Lord always!" he says. Sounds like he was a happy, carefree guy without a worry in the world, right? Wrong! Paul actually wrote this letter of Philippians from a dark, cold prison cell. That was after he had been shipwrecked twice, and beaten, and abandoned by his friends (because he chose to follow Jesus). And add to this, throughout his life Paul had some unnamed disability. Some think he might have been blind, or maybe he had leprosy or malaria. But still he writes **"Rejoice in the Lord always!"** And then, just in case his readers missed the point the first time, he writes **"I'll say it again, rejoice!"**

Rejoice always, Paul? Even when I'm hurt...even when our team got blitzed...even when I got cut from varsity...even when life is miserable at home...even when my girlfriend (or boyfriend) dumped me...even when my life is turned upside down? **Yup!** You see, Paul says that our joy doesn't come from the stuff that happens in our day-to-day lives. If that were the case, our emotions would bounce up and down like a point guard's dribble! Paul says joy comes from something deeper than that.

God loves you, friend! Your sins are forgiven...gone! You have a companion to go with you (God) throughout all of life, even when life sucks! And you have a bunch of cheerleaders (the Church) who will hold you up when the road gets a bit bumpy. Your value is not dependent upon winning...or being a superstar...or signing a college letter of intent or a pro contract. God says your are valuable because God says so!

If you haven't learned anything else in this book, I hope you've learned this: God loves you and sets you free to live. So every day is game day! God bless!

EXTRA POINT

Can you think of two or three things you learned while doing this Game Day booklet? Look over the past 24 games and find a few things that you want to work on. List them here, and then go for it!

OVERTIME

Read one of the Gospels (that's Matthew, Mark, Luke or John). Each of them is the story of Jesus' life, told from the author's point of view. (I'd suggest John)

There are 31 chapters in Proverbs (and 31 days in a month!). How about reading one each day? There's lots of great practical advice in them.

Try memorizing one or more of the verses that were in the first 25 games.

Find a friend or a teammate who might be willing to pray with you, or study the bible with you weekly.

Visit your local Christian bookstore and find books like *Comeback!* by Dave Dravecky, and other Christian athletes. They're great inspirational reading.

Ask your pastor or youth director to get some of the athletes from your church together for bible study or prayer. You might even go to a game together, or find out who the local Christian pro or college athletes are, and begin writing them. Christian athletes are often available to come to your youth group to share their faith journey.

Keep on reading, praying, thinking, and working! God has great things in store for you!

Ask a Christian teacher or coach to investigate the possibility of starting an FCA (Fellowship of Christian Athletes) group at your school.

Go through Game Day again with a group of your friends. Rather than writing your answers in Extra Point, share your thoughts and feelings out loud.

Make sure you go to church! No other single thing can enhance your faith like regular, faithful worship attendance.